LARRY BIRD

PAUL PIERCE

BOB COUSY

BILL RUSSELL

DENNIS JOHNSON

K.C. JONES

JOHN HAVLICEK

ROBERT PARISH

REGGIE LEWIS

DAVE COWENS

KEVIN McHALE

ANTOINE WALKER

CREATIVE C EDUCATION
JOHN NICHOLS

Published by Creative Education, 123 South Broad Street, Mankato, MN 56001

Creative Education is an imprint of The Creative Company.

Design and Art Direction by Rita Marshall

Photos by Allsport, AP/Wide World, NBA Photos, SportsChrome, Brian Spurlock

Library of Congress Cataloging-in-Publication Data

Nichols, John, 1966- The history of the Boston Celtics / by John Nichols.

p. cm. — (Pro basketball today)   ISBN 1-58341-091-0   1. Boston Celtics (Basketball team)—History—

Juvenile literature. [1. Boston Celtics (Basketball team)—History. 2. Basketball—History.] I. Title. II. Series.

GV885.52.B67 N53 2001   796.323'64'0974461—dc21   00-064543

First Edition 9 8 7 6 5 4 3 2 1

BOSTON, MASSACHUSETTS,

IS A CITY RICH WITH HISTORY.

PURITANS SEEKING TO ESCAPE RELIGIOUS PERSECUTION

in Europe settled there in 1630. The nation's first public school was

founded in Boston in 1635, and Alexander Graham Bell invented the

telephone there in 1876. From the first colonists to its present-day citi-

zens, Boston has been home to people and traditions that have made

America great.

Today, Boston is home to some of the nation's finest industries,

universities, and museums. One of the other points of pride among

Boston's citizens is the city's National Basketball Association (NBA)

ED MACAULEY

team. Born in 1946, the Boston Celtics were named in honor of the

city's large Irish population, and from the beginning, they captured the

The Celtics
made the
playoffs for
the first time
after the
1947–48
season despite
going 20–28.

hearts of Bostonians.

{AUERBACH LAYS THE FOUNDATION} The

Celtics tipped off their first season in 1946 playing in an

11-team league called the Basketball Association of

America (BAA). Team owner Walter Brown ran the

6 Boston Garden Arena and was a member of the National Hockey

League's Boston Bruins' front office. Brown wanted another attraction

to help fill his new arena during the winter months, and the Celtics

were born. The team played three seasons in the BAA before the league

merged with a rival league to form the NBA in 1949.

The Celtics' first four seasons were losing ones, but in 1950, things

began to change. That year, the Celtics hired a brash young coach by the

DANNY AINGE

Guard Bill Sharman led the Celtics in scoring for four straight seasons in the late **1950s**.

BILL SHARMAN

name of Arnold "Red" Auerbach. Auerbach quickly taught the Celtics

that he would not tolerate losing, and that winning could be achieved

only through teamwork.

Auerbach quickly reshaped his roster, adding young

talents such as point guard Bob Cousy, shooting guard

Bill Sharman, and forward Chuck Cooper. Of these play-

ers, Cousy made the biggest impact. The flashy 6-foot-1

dynamo could handle the ball like it was strung to his finger, and his

style of passing was so deceptive that surprised teammates were often

hit in the face with the ball. "Cousy was the catalyst for our team," said

Auerbach. "He drove the guys to play their best."

From 1950–51 to 1955–56, the Celtics made the playoffs every

year. But despite their success, Auerbach knew that his Celtics needed

one more player to make them a true contender. "We needed a big

Forward Chuck Cooper, the NBA's first black player, was one of Boston's first great rebounders.

CHUCK COOPER

With center Bill Russell manning the middle, the Celtics ruled the NBA for more than a decade.

BILL RUSSELL

defender in order to get over the top," noted the fiery coach.

Fortunately for Boston fans, Auerbach already had a big man in mind

who would fit the bill.

Guard Frank Ramsey's great outside shooting helped Boston win the **1957** championship.

{RUSSELL LEADS THE CHARGE} In the 1956 NBA Draft, the Celtics traded forward Ed Macauley and another young player to the St. Louis Hawks for the right to draft an athletic center from the University of San

Francisco by the name of Bill Russell. Auerbach was convinced that Russell was the missing piece to the Celtics' championship puzzle, and it didn't take long for Russell to prove his new coach right. The 6-foot-9 and 220-pound rookie prowled the lane aggressively, blocking shots and pulling down rebounds at a remarkable pace.

Behind their big man, the 1956–57 Celtics went 44–28 and tore through the playoffs to face the St. Louis Hawks in the NBA Finals.

TOM HEINSOHN

After six hard-fought games, the series was deadlocked. The deciding

game seven was a classic struggle. The Celtics and Hawks battled

through two overtimes before Boston finally pulled out a 125–123 vic-

tory to claim its first NBA championship. "It was amazing for a team so

young to play so well," said a smiling Auerbach, victory cigar in hand.

"This team has a great future."

Auerbach proved to be a prophet. With Russell and Cousy providing the leadership, potent talents such as guards K.C. Jones and Sam

The Celtics set a team record with 107 rebounds in a **1960** playoff game against Philadelphia.

Jones and forwards Tom Heinsohn and Tom "Satch" Sanders delivered much of the team's punch. The Celtics rolled to an incredible nine world championships in the next 10 years. It was one of the most dominant runs in the history of professional sports, and at the center of it all was

14

the legendary Bill Russell.

During the Celtics' magical run, the cat-quick Russell averaged more than 16 points, 23 rebounds, and 4 assists per game. He also won the league's Most Valuable Player award five times. Russell's single-minded devotion to winning kept the talented Celtics working together with machine-like precision. "Russell was the greatest competitor I ever coached," said Auerbach.

BOB COUSY

After the 1965–66 championship season, Auerbach retired from

coaching and moved to the front office. To replace him, the Celtics

turned to Bill Russell, who accepted the dual role of player-coach and

became the first African-American coach in NBA history. During

Russell's three years at the helm, the Celtics won two more NBA cham-

pionships, including one in 1968–69, Russell's final season as a Celtics player and coach. Just four years later, the center was inducted into the

Basketball Hall of Fame.

{THE TRADITION LIVES ON} Boston's first season after Bill Russell's retirement yielded a mere 34–48 record. All at once, the magic of the team's home court, the Boston Garden, seemed to disappear. Many experts thought the Celtics were in for a long period of rebuilding under new coach Tom Heinsohn.

Guard K.C. Jones had his finest season in **1965–66**, leading Boston with six assists per game.

Fortunately for Celtics fans, the team was not rebuilding—it was simply reloading. By the 1970–71 season, talented young players such as brawny center Dave Cowens and sweet-shooting guard Jo Jo White were added to a lineup that already featured All-Star forward John Havlicek. The Celtics rose quickly, and by 1973, the team was once again among the league's elite.

K.C. JONES

Stars such as
Robert Parish
helped the
Celtics cast a
giant shadow
across the NBA
for decades.

The new Celtics powerhouse reminded many fans of the championship teams of the '60s. Both featured a hustling, relentless style that

wore down opponents and forced mistakes. Cowens, Havlicek, and White seemed to step right in where Russell, Sam Jones, and Cousy had left off. "We play Celtics basketball," explained Havlicek. "We work hard every night and we don't care who gets the glory. It's all

about the team."

In 1973–74, Cowens's rebounding, Havlicek's scoring, and White's smooth ball handling propelled the Celtics to a 56–26 record and a playoff berth. After knocking out the Buffalo Braves and the New York Knicks, Boston faced the Milwaukee Bucks for the NBA championship.

The Bucks were led by the league's most dominant big man, Kareem Abdul-Jabbar, but the Celtics countered with their trademark

JOHN HAVLICEK

balanced attack. After six games, the series stood tied. In game seven,

Cowens erupted for 28 points to lead the Celtics to a 102–87 victory

and the franchise's 12th NBA title.

In 1976, Cowens, Havlicek, and White led Boston to championship

heights once more, winning a thrilling NBA Finals series against the

Phoenix Suns. The 35-year-old Havlicek, though hobbled by a leg injury, led the charge once more. Two years later, the 13-time All-Star retired,

signaling the end of another great era of Celtics basketball. "Nobody

ever played this game harder than Havlicek," noted team-

mate Don Nelson. "He was as tough as they come."

{BOSTON SOARS WITH BIRD} In the 1979 NBA

Draft, Boston used its first-round selection to take Larry

Bird, a forward from Indiana State University. The 6-foot-

9 Bird had been a major star in college, but many experts thought he

was too slow and unathletic to be a major force in the NBA. The Celtics

thought otherwise. "Larry doesn't wow you with physical skills," noted

new coach Bill Fitch. "But he's the best fundamental basketball player

I've ever seen."

The Celtics also engineered some shrewd trades to acquire point

guard Nate "Tiny" Archibald and center Robert Parish to complement

Small but speedy guard Nate Archibald triggered Boston's offense in the early **1980s**.

NATE ARCHIBALD

Larry Bird's intelligence and deadly shooting made him an NBA legend in the **1980s**.

LARRY BIRD

Bird and young forward Cedric "Cornbread" Maxwell. In the 1980

Draft, the Celtics struck gold yet again, acquiring 6-foot-11 power for-

ward Kevin McHale. With this wealth of talent in place, Kevin McHale

featured a

the Celtics were back in business. soft hook

shot and

In 1980–81, the recharged Celtics barreled through superb funda-

mental skills

the regular season with a 62–20 mark. Bird's 21 points in the low

per game fueled the offense, while the defense of Parish, post.

McHale, and Maxwell stopped opposing teams dead in their tracks. The

Celtics stormed to the NBA Finals, where they met the Houston

Rockets and their star center, Moses Malone. The Celtics' swarm of stars

overwhelmed the scrappy Rockets in six games, and Boston was a cham-

pion once more.

Two seasons later, Bill Fitch was replaced as head coach by K.C.

Jones. Coach Jones wasted no time in revamping the team's attack, trad-

KEVIN McHALE

ing for All-Star guard Dennis Johnson in an effort to strengthen the

team's defense and add more scoring punch. The move paid immediate

dividends as Boston rolled to yet another championship. The victim this

time was the Los Angeles Lakers and their star guard, Magic Johnson.

Bird and the Celtics claimed yet another NBA championship in

1986, dispatching the Houston Rockets in six games. "Larry Legend," as the Celtics' faithful called the star forward, led Boston's charge until

1992, when chronic back problems forced him to retire. Bird finished

with the amazing career averages of 24 points, 10

rebounds, and 6 assists per game—numbers that made

him a lock for the Hall of Fame.

{TRAGEDY HITS THE CELTICS} Among the

Celtics' many traditional strengths was their ability to

Dennis Johnson ran Boston's offense as the Celtics beat the Lakers for the **1984** championship.

replace aging stars with new talent. From Russell to Havlicek to Bird,

Boston was always able to find the next great player just over the horizon.

Unfortunately, in the mid-1980s, the team's fortunes began to change.

In 1986, the Celtics drafted a standout forward named Len Bias,

expecting the former University of Maryland star to carry Boston to yet

another era of championship basketball. Unfortunately, Bias never got

the chance. The 21-year-old died shortly after the draft as a result of a

DENNIS JOHNSON

drug overdose. "Lenny Bias was a phenomenal talent," said Celtics team president Red Auerbach. "He could do it all."

In his last season **(1992–93)**, Reggie Lewis paced Boston with almost 21 points a game.

The next year, Boston spent its top draft pick on Reggie Lewis, a multitalented forward from Boston's own Northeastern University. The 6-foot-8 Lewis instantly brought youthful energy and enthusiasm to the veteran Celtics lineup. "Reggie gives us a guy who can explode to the basket and make things happen," observed Larry Bird.

By 1992, Lewis was an All-Star and the rightful heir to Bird's throne as the leader of the Celtics. But in the 1993 playoffs, during the Celtics' first game against the Charlotte Hornets, Lewis suddenly collapsed on the court. Diagnosed with an irregular heartbeat, he missed the rest of the playoffs. During the off-season, he collapsed again while shooting baskets and died of a heart attack. The twin tragedies deprived

REGGIE LEWIS

the Celtics of the two stars they had counted on to lead the team into the post-Bird era.

{PITINO TAKES THE REINS} After losing Bias and Lewis, the Celtics suffered through several subpar seasons. Not since the 1940s had Boston suffered as many as three consecutive losing seasons. By the end of the 1996–97 season, the team had endured four straight.

Hardworking forward Dino Radja anchored the Celtics' frontcourt in the mid-**1990s**.

Looking to rebuild, the Celtics hired Rick Pitino as their new head coach and team president. Pitino had built a reputation as a winner when he coached the New York Knicks and the University of Kentucky Wildcats before joining Boston. In both instances, he used a sharp eye for talent and a keen mind for strategy to revive teams that had fallen on hard times. "I plan to work harder than anybody can imagine to get the Celtics back on top," proclaimed Pitino.

DINO RADJA

A quick first step and great athleticism made young forward Paul Pierce a rising star.

PAUL PIERCE

Antoine Walker was the Celtics' top scorer and rebounder from **1996–97** to **1999–00**.

ANTOINE WALKER

Slowly but surely, the hard-driving coach put his stamp on the team. Over the course of three seasons in Boston, Pitino transformed an aging Celtics club into one of the league's youngest and most aggressive. Young players such as forwards Antoine Walker and Paul Pierce and center Vitaly Potapenko showed flashes of brilliance but also struggled while adjusting to the pro game. "Our team is so young,"

observed Pitino during the 1999–00 season. "They're going to make mistakes, but we're in it for the long haul. These guys are our future."

The Celtics' tradition is one that demands excellence. A history that includes a record 16 NBA titles cannot be ignored. But the journey to more championships must begin with a first step. Spurred on by Boston's loyal fans and a desire for greatness, today's team hopes to recreate the days when the mighty Celtics ruled the NBA.

Celtics fans hoped that forward Tony Battie would become the team's next great shot blocker.

TONY BATTIE